Start-Up
Connections

THE GREAT FIRE
OF LONDON

Stewart Ross

Evans

ted

First published in this edition in 2010

Published by Evans Brothers Limited
2A Portman Mansions
Chiltern Street
London W1U 6NR

Produced for Evans Brothers Limited by
White-Thomson Publishing Ltd.,
+44 (0) 843 2087 460
www.wtpub.co.uk

Printed & bound in China by New Era Printing
Company Limited

Editor: Dereen Taylor
Consultants: Nina Siddall, Head of Primary School
Improvement, East Sussex; Norah Granger, former
primary head teacher and senior lecturer in Education,
University of Brighton; Kate Ruttle, freelance literacy
consultant and Literacy Co-ordinator, Special Needs
Co-ordinator, and Deputy Headteacher at a primary
school in Suffolk.
Designer: Leishman Design
Cover design: Balley Design Limited

British Library Cataloguing in Publication Data

Ross, Stewart
    The Great Fire of London. -- (Start-up connections)
    1. Great Fire, London, England, 1666--Juvenile literature.
    2. London (England)--History--17th century--Juvenile
    literature.
    I. Title II. Series
    942.1'066-dc22

ISBN: 978 0 237 54169 9

Picture Acknowledgements: Bridgeman Art Library/
Gavin Graham Gallery 5; Bridgeman Art Library/Museum
of London 7 (bottom); Bridgeman Art Library/
Corporation of London 19; Bridgeman Art Library/
O'Shea Gallery, London 18-19; Bridgeman Art Library/
Private Collection (cover, centre), (title page), 4, 4-5, 18
(top); Bridgeman Art Library/Royal Society of Arts 8 (top);
Bridgeman Art Library/Simon Carter Gallery 7 (top);
Mary Evans Picture Library 10, 11; Museum of London
16-17; Pepys Library, Magdalene College, Cambridge
(cover, top right), 8 (bottom); Piers Cavendish/Impact 13;
The National Portrait Gallery 9; Topham Picturepoint 12,
15; Topham Picturepoint/London Fire Brigade Museum
(cover, top left), 14.

Contents

The Great Fire of London

▼ A very long time ago, London looked like this.

The old city of London was burned in a great fire. This happened almost 350 years ago.

ago   old   burned   fire   years

▼ These people watched the flames from boats on the River Thames.

After the fire, the city was rebuilt.

▲ This Monument was built so that people remember the Great Fire.
It is still standing today.

flames   river   rebuilt   today   5

When was the Great Fire of London?

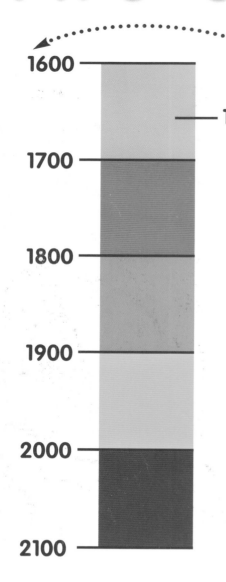

1600
1666
1700
1800
1900
2000
2100

These numbers are years.
We also call them dates.
What is the date today?

100 years is called a century.
In the timeline each century
is a different colour.

The Great Fire of London
was in the year 1666.

dates   century

◄ **This is King Charles II. He was the King of England in 1666.**

▼ **Here is a painting of the fire. Is it night-time or daytime? Paintings like this tell us about the fire.**

timeline   painting

How do we know about the Great Fire?

▶ **This is Samuel Pepys. He lived in London at the time of the Great Fire. He wrote about the fire in his diary.**

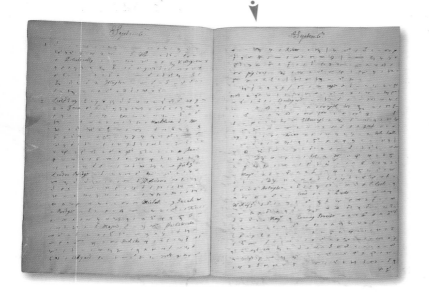

"It made me weep to see it. The churches, houses, and all on fire and flaming at once, and a horrid noise the flames made."

diary   churches

This is John Evelyn. He also wrote about the fire in his diary.

"By night it was light as day for ten miles round about."

People who watch an event are called 'eyewitnesses'. Samuel Pepys and John Evelyn were eyewitnesses to the Great Fire.

houses   miles   eyewitnesses

How did the Great Fire start?

The Great Fire **began** with a little fire in a **bakery**.

The bakery was in a street called Pudding Lane.

In this picture of a bakery from the **past**, the fire is for the **oven**.

began   bakery   past

The houses of old London
were very close to each other.
How did the fire spread from
the bakery to other houses?

oven   spread

Why did a little fire become the Great Fire?

These houses are from the time of the Great Fire.

They are built with wood frames.
We call them timber-framed.

wood   timber-framed

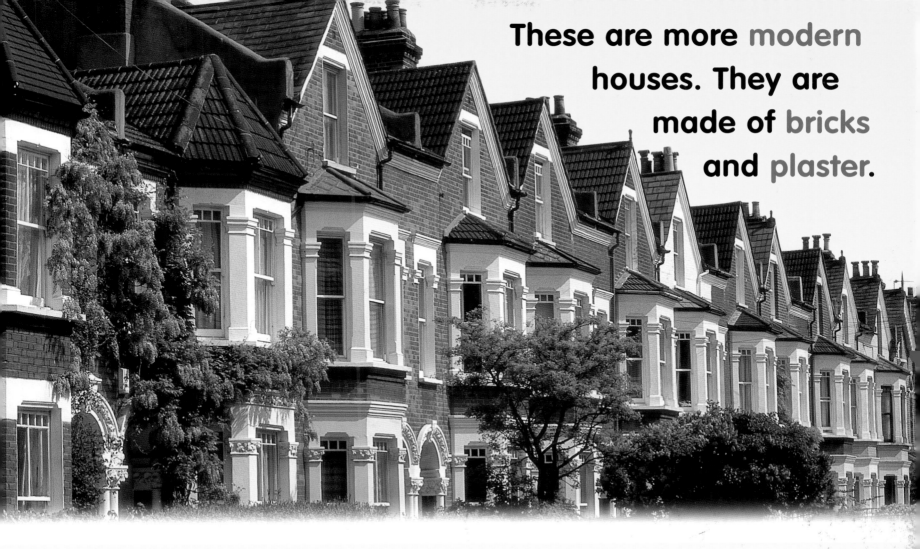

These are more modern houses. They are made of bricks and plaster.

Which burns best, brick or wood?

In the Great Fire the wind sent the flames from one house to another.

Pepys thought the fire would reach his house.

He moved out.

modern   bricks   plaster   wind   13

Trying to put out the fire

There was no fire brigade at the time of the Great Fire.

People had to carry water from the River Thames in buckets. It took a long time.

They could not put out the big fire.

fire brigade   buckets

◀ **Modern fire-fighters have fire engines to carry their hoses and ladders. They can stop a fire spreading to other houses.**

fire-fighters engines hoses ladders **15**

After the Great Fire

**The Great Fire of London lasted for five days.
It burned 13,200 houses.**

**The top picture shows what London looked like
before the fire.**

lasted **before**

The bottom picture shows what it looked like afterwards.

Many people had no homes.
Pepys' house was not burned down.

You can see that many churches were still standing.
Why were they not destroyed?

afterwards   homes   destroyed

Building a new city

▼ **This is Christopher Wren. He planned a pleasant new London with wide streets and houses of stone and brick.**

The old London was crowded and dirty. The new city was cleaner and healthier.

planned   streets   stone   crowded

▼ Before the fire,
St Paul's Cathedral
was the most
famous building in
all London. After the
fire, it was a ruin.

▲ Christopher Wren built this
new St Paul's Cathedral.
How is it different from
the old one?
It is still standing today,
but parts of it have changed.

dirty   cleaner   healthier   ruin

The story of

Here is a map of London in 1666. The yellow, orange and red areas burned down.

Use these pictures to tell the story of the Great Fire.

KEY

	London
	Area burned on Sunday, 2nd September, 1666
	Area burned on Monday, 3rd September, 1666
	Area burned on Tuesday/Wednesday, 4/5th September, 1666
	London Wall, which was built long ago and surrounded the city of London.

ALDERSGATE STREET

HOLBORN

FETTER LANE

LUDGATE HILL

St Paul's Cathedral

RIVER

the Great Fire

N
W E
S

0   250   500
metres

BISHOPSGATE STREET

WHITECHAPEL

CHEAPSIDE

CORNHILL

LOMBARD STREET

SEETHING LANE
(Pepys's street)

TOWER STREET

THAMES STREET

The Tower
of
London

LONDON BRIDGE

PUDDING LANE

THAMES

Further information for Parents and Teachers

THE GREAT FIRE OF LONDON ACTIVITY PAGE

Use the activities on these pages to help you to make the most of The Great Fire of London in your classroom.

Activities suggested on this page support progression in learning by consolidating and developing ideas from the book and helping the children to link the new concepts with their own experiences. Making these links is crucial in helping young children to engage with learning and to become lifelong learners.

Ideas on the next page develop essential skills for learning by suggesting ways of making links across the curriculum and in particular to literacy, numeracy and ICT.

WORD PANEL

Check that the children know the meaning of each of these words from the book.

afterwards	crowded	planned	timber-framed
ago	diary	plaster	timeline
before	eyewitness	rebuilt	timeline
bricks	modern	ruin	today
century	old	stone	wooden
church	past		years

PAINTINGS AND DIARIES.

Use the diary extracts and contemporary pictures in the book, as well as those on the internet, to discuss how we know about things that happened in the past.

- Check that children have an understanding of the idea of 'past'. A walking timeline can be helpful: children take a step down a corridor/hall/playground and mark the place at the time when they were born. Another two or three steps will show when their parents were born. Then mark in their grandparents' births. Keep taking steps back to mark other significant historical events the children know about.
- Explain why there are no photographs or video footage of the Great Fire.
  Reread the diary extracts while the children look at the pictures.
- Discuss the different kinds of information recorded in each source.

- Which do the children find more interesting to use?
  Ask children to take photographs, draw pictures and write a diary about your 'walking timeline'. Compare the information.

BUILDING THEN AND NOW

Introduce children to the houses in your local area. How you do this will depend on facilities available locally

- Visit an estate agent, either locally or on the internet, so you can 'see inside' different types of houses in the local area.
- Use photographs of houses to discuss building materials. Help the children to distinguish between brick, stone and timber-framed. Look at roofs, roofing materials and chimneys. Talk about the different kinds of windows. Help the children to develop vocabulary to talk about the buildings.
- Talk about ways of finding out, or guessing, when the house might have been built. Is it 'modern', 'older' or 'very old'?
- Take the children out on a walk around the area. Give them digital cameras to take photographs of interesting buildings.
- Back in school, ask children to write observations about the buildings they photographed.
  - What is the building used for?
  - What are the building materials?
  - What is the roof like?
  - Is the building 'modern', 'older' or 'very old'?

FIREFIGHTERS

Ask firefighters from the local fire station to visit the school and give the children a talk on fire safety. Ideally, ask them to bring their fire engines.

- Before the visit, talk about questions the children might want to ask.
- Warn the children that the firefighters might ask them questions too.
- If the firefighters are willing, they may supervise the burning of your model street so that the children can see how leaving gaps between buildings is one way to stop the progress of a fire.

USING THE GREAT FIRE OF LONDON FOR CROSS CURRICULAR WORK

The revised national curriculum focuses on children developing key competencies as

- successful learners
- confident individuals and
- responsible citizens.

Cross curricular work is particularly beneficial in developing the thinking and learning skills that contribute to building these competencies because it encourages children to make links, to transfer learning skills and to apply knowledge from one context to another. As importantly, cross curricular work can help children to understand how school work links to their daily lives. For many children, this is a key motivation in becoming a learner.

The web below indicates some areas for cross curricular study. Others may well come from your own class's engagement with the ideas in the book.

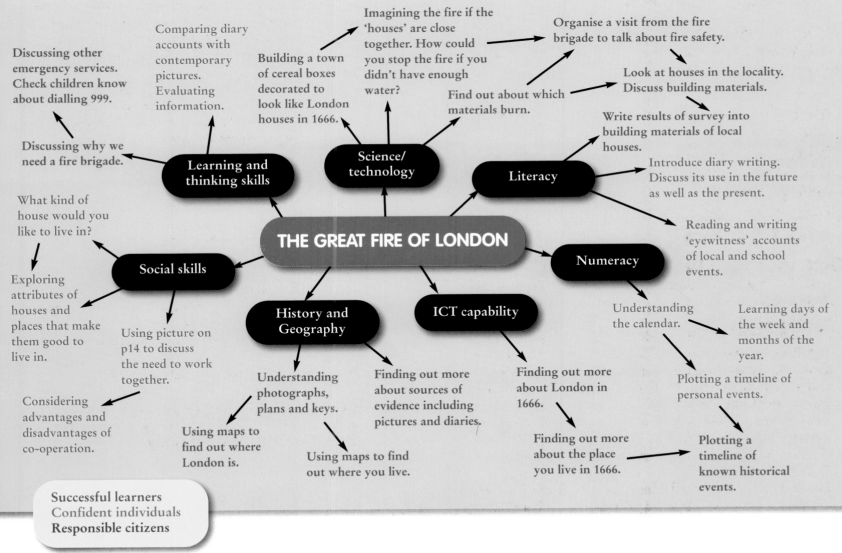

THE GREAT FIRE OF LONDON

Discussing other emergency services. Check children know about dialling 999.

Comparing diary accounts with contemporary pictures. Evaluating information.

Building a town of cereal boxes decorated to look like London houses in 1666.

Imagining the fire if the 'houses' are close together. How could you stop the fire if you didn't have enough water?

Organise a visit from the fire brigade to talk about fire safety.

Discussing why we need a fire brigade.

Find out about which materials burn.

Look at houses in the locality. Discuss building materials.

Write results of survey into building materials of local houses.

Learning and thinking skills

Science/technology

Literacy

Introduce diary writing. Discuss its use in the future as well as the present.

What kind of house would you like to live in?

Reading and writing 'eyewitness' accounts of local and school events.

Exploring attributes of houses and places that make them good to live in.

Social skills

Numeracy

Using picture on p14 to discuss the need to work together.

History and Geography

ICT capability

Understanding the calendar.

Learning days of the week and months of the year.

Considering advantages and disadvantages of co-operation.

Understanding photographs, plans and keys.

Finding out more about sources of evidence including pictures and diaries.

Finding out more about London in 1666.

Plotting a timeline of personal events.

Using maps to find out where London is.

Using maps to find out where you live.

Finding out more about the place you live in 1666.

Plotting a timeline of known historical events.

Successful learners
Confident individuals
Responsible citizens

Index